The Storyteller of Isfahan

by Robert Hale

Published by
YABISA GASHOUSE
C/ R. Curtoys Gotarredona, 1, Esc. 2, 2B
07840 Santa Eulària des Riu
Spain

ISBN: 978-84-949638-2-7

Find Robert Hale's poetry at:
www.roberthalepoetry.wordpress.com
www.nobettertimethanthis.tumblr.com
www.instagram.com/roberthale.poetry

And strange at Ecbatan the trees
Take leaf by leaf the evening strange
The flooding dark about their knees
The mountains over Persia change

From *You, Andrew Marvell* by Archibald MacLeish in *Collected Poems 1917-1952* (Houghton Mifflin Company, 1952). Reproduced with permission from Houghton Mifflin Harcourt.

Foreword

This is my second collection of verse[1]. With few exceptions, these poems were written over the course of the past year. My poems continue to be inspired by the beauty of nature, particularly that of my home island of Ibiza, by human behaviour and the human condition, the mystery of the world and our perception of it, and the eternal theme of love. I hope you enjoy these new poems.

Santa Eulària des Riu, Eivissa[2], 28/12/18

---

1 My first poetry book was *No Better Time than This*, independently published on CreateSpace Independent Publishing Platform, 2018, republished by Yabisa gashouse, 2019.

2 Eivissa is the local name for Ibiza, where a dialect of Catalan is spoken.

Contents

To my wife, my children, my parents.
To my true friends.
To the wind and the clouds, the sun, moon and stars, the sky itself, the hills, forests and wild flowers, the sea, lakes, rivers and streams, the earth beneath my feet.
To the poets of Yabisa Gashouse.
To the true mystics.

A song of love to Clouds Woman...

Since Ever I Was Touched by Your Eyes

Spoke the wind to me as words will not tell
Before ever I knew or better, understood
That she
Had touched me to my quick
Changed the rhythm, the essence of my days
Full again did I run and leap
Living again by ultimate law
Benumbed by ultimate wonder
Moved by ultimate mystery
My beloved is she
Who is sweet air for my lungs
Who is the beating heart in my chest
Who is blood coursing through my veins
Red as the rose flower on her breast
Which I picked in the morning
Strong as the wind which took my soul
And blew it with her own
But soft as ever I would touch her skin
A garden to me is my beloved
I lie amongst the blossoms of spring
The blooms of summer
Of fragrance intoxicating
As sweet as the scent off her skin
Upon the moon of May I wished a wish
Renewed on each new day
Since ever I was touched by her eyes

ROBERT HALE

Santa Eulària des Riu, Eivissa, 2002.

The theme of leaving has exercised poets and songsters down through the countless ages of thinking, feeling, creative humankind. Here are two poems on that eternal theme. Imagine, if you will, the poet is on a ferry heading north one bleak, leaden, winter evening. A dark strip of land appears and grows wider over to the port side. An hour left to destination, separated by a sea from lighter lands and a love left behind…

Leaving in February

A white wake trailed aft, dead straight
Ahead, a sky the colour of forget-me-nots
As we made the south-east corner
On a morning.

I shall remember that leaving
Over and over.
As if I am already remembering tomorrow.

Every mile advanced, my spirit has bled
Dark drops to the wake.
A thin line of brooding hills, suddenly visible
Distant against a Northern sky
Upon an evening.

From out of a leaden sky the sun
Spills molten to the pewter sea.

A dream too vivid, too recurrent.
Still I look to see Her turn
To wave the last wave.

Mediterranean Sea, near Barcelona, February 2002.

Night Bird

It is sad my love to come away
When the trees stand bent and black
The night bird sleeps, a deep fog creeps
Cold on the boundless flat
Remember its call on the velvet night
But there! The night bird weeps
Its dreams abound in the rush of light
That from coming spring must leap
Oh, to lie with you again my love
To hear the night bird sing
To fill our minds with the light that
     blinds
With you soft against my skin

Mediterranean Sea, near Barcelona, December 2003.

I hear so many middle-aged people blaming their parents for the bad things in their lives. But growing up means, at a certain point, accepting responsibility for your own life, whatever. Being a parent is perhaps the most difficult job there is, and there's no reliable map. For myself, I have only admiration for my own parents' negotiations with some of the troubles I presented them with...

Becoming Worthy Again

Black oblongs, spitting orange fire
Break an early skyline, yellow pale
With dull blue-grey, through a windowpane
Of the green train to Fenchurch Street.

Ber-dum ber-dum, berd-um berd-um,
And the the wheels hissing hard on the rails.

Dad with big brother, on the opposite seat,
Leaning in, says, that's where they make
Petrol to make the cars and lorries go.
I am wounded, and when later I ask,
"Why do you tell him things, but not me?",
He is wounded, too.
And after that tells me things, too.

You learn a first hurt never can be small,
That sickly feeling, leaves a hidden scar
That's tender, even after healing.

Dad holds his second born son
For in-law Mum and Dad to see

(They who would bounce him on their knee),
And all look happy and proud and gay
In a photo, in black and white and grey.
(The second born is me).
Here I am new, ugly, wet and bald;
How proud Dad must have been again
Later when he saw me sit and crawl!
But things get complicated then.

Big brother and I caught hell when we stood
On the radiator Dad had fixed
To the bathroom wall,
And it came crashing down; Because
Dad said don't climb on it at all,
And we did.
A fury we hadn't known before,
And maybe neither had Dad, who
I only later knew, was sorry,
And carried his wound with him too.

Considering this, that one once was worthy,
Yet after the wounds and pain,
(Though seemingly banal),
How can one become it again?

It does not help when, a not-quite teenager,
And in truth, a little shit,
Dad must take tools with best friend's Dad
To mend a fence you wrecked (with kicks).
Nor does it help if you drive your first
Honda CD one-seven-five into the garage
        door

The very first time you power it up,
Bending it a bit. (Oh, how he swore!)
Dad's face was black, his words were fire.
You could not know Dad's anguish then,
But you did, his ire.

Having said that, he did not make a drama
      when
You were not eating and got thin,
Or set off to India at nineteen,
Although you have to admit that when
You turned down a good job and a PhD,
To go off and teach in Italy,
He wasn't all that happy.
To understate the matter.

Dad said he stood on the right of Atilla
The Hun. He was not wrong, ever,
But often, also, he was fun.

Now the years have gone, and so too, his leg -
Not literally - but wasted, it won't carry him
Across the lawn to his beloved shed.
And even if it could, that would be in vain:
His hands won't grip his tools, nor work his
      wood,
Nor even feel its grain.

Yet now he produces things I never thought
      I'd see:
Patience, stoicism, philosophy.
He finds to do and is content. But more:
For all the questionable acts, disagreed-with

    decisions,
Radiator falls, garage door collisions,
Misunderstandings on a train
In the pale early morn
You see him mellow, and you see again
In his eyes, a pride,
For his second born.

Considering this - and life's a complicated
    story -
You find the two of you have all along
Been of each other worthy.

Santa Eulària des Riu, Eivissa, December 2016.

A true story about a magical object...

The Cocktail Shaker

She had taken it down to clean
but hadn't got round to it yet,
(like so many other things)
so it stood with polish and rags
on the little Turkish table
by the sofa where he sits
now beside her.

It had woven in and out of her life
like a shuttle through warp
for forty years and more.
She says
it's not just any old bit of tin,
she fancies it contains a jinn
which moves it hither and thither
according to circumstance and whim.
Now it is old and the silver is black.
And now he is here and wanting to look.

He turns its silver casing
and reads
'A' for Alexander: Gin,
Crème de cacao, Cream
One measure each.
She likes things with chocolate cream
but prefers a brandy drink to gin.
That's an Alexander Number 2

(a Brandy Alexander, to you).

But brandy's good with soda and ice.
Have you tried it? she asks, It's nice.
For forty years at witching hour,
after sunset at seven or eight
depending on the latitude,
she'd poured herself one
(or two if it got late)
ever since a young man out East
bought her one to try (at least).
She says it hits the spot.
Long ago and far away,
she says,
That was another day.

And today is a day for something new
He says, and so, with jacket on,
goes to look for crème de cacao,
finds it somewhere, somehow,
takes the shaker to the kitchen.
Pouring, clinking, ice rattling, liquor swishing.
Oh, what memories it brings!
(All a bit mixed up, she says,
like the liquor and ice and things.)
Shake, shake, shake,
shake, shake, and pour
gold-white velvet in a glass.
Here's yours.
Sits on the sofa beside her,
they take a sip, he gives
a penny for her thoughts.

And her thought is this feels a little
like a beginning, how strange.
She looks far away, thinks of her age,
And isn't it odd, she thinks to the jinn,
How things begin? And the jinn
brings her a thought, on a whim.

She goes to the shelf above the phone,
takes down a photo in a frame,
sits with him again.
Eyes glancing bright, with such a light,
as he would remember, then
hands him the picture to see.

A dark-skinned woman stands, shapeless,
in white smock, loose black trousers,
black hair pulled tight in a bun,
a bangle on her wrist,
something white in her hand.
For the photo, slightly turned,
looking to one side, a kind
half-smile on her face.

Beside her, on a little table
sitting in a party frock
shiny sandals, long white socks
bandy legs hanging free,
hair black, cut short,
straight fringe, just combed.
Dark eyes wide in puppy-fat,
puzzled, anxious, looks off camera,
arm held tightly by her *amah*.

So long ago and far away,
quietly she says again.
He looks to her now, searches for
the little girl in the picture frame.
But she is far away,
reflecting on the letter 'A'.
'A' for Alexander, 'A' for *Amah*
'A' for *Amore*, of which
there have been quite a few.
(She is no beginner.)

It was at the restaurant down below
with this same man, not so long ago,
that another beginning - a source, perhaps
of new weft for some remaining warp
unaccountably was brought
to be on a whim by the jinn,
in the cocktail shaker
on the Turkish table
by the sofa
where he sits now beside her
She looks back at him, and wonders
what he sees
within.

Santa Eulària des Riu, Eivissa, December 2016.

I have known this small town in the north-east of Italy for many years. On Friday mornings the market comes to town...

Corso Vittorio Emanuelle II, Market Day

Country people come to town
Rumpled, drably crumpled
In fraying Friday best
Town women in boutique fashion
Cruise the sidewalks by the stalls
Feigning disinterest when he calls
I've lots of nice things just in
Ma guardi che bellin
Signora!

Older ladies bustle in furs
Voices rough as the winter earth
Thick make-up plasters cracks in time
In faces sour as home-made wine
Eyes heavy as the day
Yet sharp as shards
Like vultures homing on their prey
And hands quick to sift and bag
The finest new-in bargain rags

The not-so simpleton by the church
Humming psalms, taking alms
From pious people gone to mass
Smiles at the kids, then says gee whizz,
Old Bepe left us in the night

And women walking by
Stop and look at the necrologue
Stand and read it like a book
Tut-tutting in the cold damp fog
Then nod to the poor man
Bumbling at the door and
Slip in to the coffee house next door
For rich hot chocolate
And wicked gossip
To keep the brain alive

Outside people mill and throng
By the cheese van, the smell is strong
And the sellers all have milk-white skin
And on the steps of the "Alpin"
Are the flower stalls where the scent is sweet
And the trade is brisk, and then they meet
At the bar above, in the archway
And they talk of how the business goes
And they talk of the politics of the day
And two chihuahuas trot along
In tartan-patterned winter coats
At a hundred euros each a throw
And a pooch is carried in mamma's arms
She asks, do you want to be let down?
And her husband puts it on the ground
So, apparently, it said yes
That's my guess
Anyway

On the station road the simple
Simpleton walks away his life

Big and clumsy, darkly pimpled
Waddling, swaying as he goes
God knows
These streets are his
Where all his story has been told
Where through the years
I've watched him growing old
He throws his fag end to the slabs
Greets friends who do not answer back
Ciao Gianni, Piero, come va?
Pretends he is like them, what then?
Ciao ragazzi, ciao ciao, ciao ciao
What now?
Bum a cigarette, some change
Do the rounds
And round again
Another market day

A small town in north-eastern Italy, December 2017.

In my first volume of poetry, *No Better Time than This*, appeared a poem I wrote in the 1990s about the Balkan war. I commented that it was still topical because for "Sarajevo" you might just as well read "Aleppo" and it would be much the same. Then, after reading a newspaper report, I wrote this...

Aleppo

The children walk to school
Hands held in mothers'
The cold December rain
Collects in crater bottoms
Turns broken streets to mud
And guns still sound just half a mile away

We haven't had lessons since the bombs began
Maryam explains,
We have learned nothing, she says
Maryam is nine, and wise
But oh, they have learned so much
Of fire and fear and death
And the messy details
Of human anatomy
Oh yes, they know about war
They are the experts

There is hope
There are no more shells
Everyday the gunfire is less
Spring will bring green shoots
Unfurling through burnt soil
Reaching up through rubble

For light and life
Even now
Human business is wriggling back into shape
Knocked badly out of step
But its deeper rhythm unstopped
Unstoppable

Mothers walking children to school
Cucumbers on a roadside stall
Families returning to pockmarked homes
Cluster in the room that's left
Begin to assemble
Order from chaos
Life goes on
Except for whom it didn't
Like Maryam
Extinguished by a last stray bullet
On her way to school
But the gravest death of all is seen
In Mohmmad's eyes
He watched
As his own light died

Santa Eulària des Riu, Eivissa, January 2018.

When I was teaching (osteopathy, since you ask), I always told my students, "When I tell you something, get used to asking me how I know". Think of some fact that you think you know. How do you know? How reliable is your source? Are you sure?

Truth

Folklore and tradition
Faith and superstition
Astrology, cosmology
Chinese numerology
Opinion, authority
Alternative philosophy
Principles and practices
Logical analysis
Sound common sense
Intellectual pretence
Induction, deduction
Cartesian reduction
Rules of thumb, heuristics,
Probability and statistics
Magical potions
Heartfelt emotions
Fallacy and heresy
Intellectual jealousy
Convention, orthodoxy
Argument by proxy
Default position, precognition
Dogmatic repetition
Experience, experiments
Divine omniscience
Fantastical imagination

Expedient interpretation
Extraordinary intuition
Unfounded supposition
Absolute and finite
Relative, indefinite
Post truth, fake news
All views[3], says who?
Ideas are very sticky
Truth is very tricky

Santa Eulària des Riu, Eivissa, January 2018.

---

3   "All views" was at the time of writing a slogan of Euronews, a European news broadcaster. That was before they changed their format to that brash, flash, American news network style.

You will have witnessed this kind of immensely sad situation, too, I am sure. A couple sitting together at a bar or restaurant table but not speaking to each other, hardly looking at each other, obviously bored with each other's company, and their life together...

The Wrong Kind of Death

Through the stark vastness of window glass
To the void of a night-time February street
There is nothing, but she does not look
Just a mirror, but she dare not see -
To examine it gets just too bleak
There is nothing, there, any more
She will not look and does not speak

A waiter, a glass of water on a tray
For her, a beer for him,
She looks about the room, looks to the street
Looks to the awful window glass, the marks
Of all dried up raindrops past
He looks at his beer, at the door, at his feet
He stares at his beer, he does not speak

Middle age passes like that lone white van
On the street. Her face, once winning
Bright smiling on a bright wedding day
In May, now
Is pickle-sour
His is a greying piece of card, a menu
Unchanging, with nothing to choose
And the van goes on its way

An inch-thick dirty raindrop spotted pane
Three yards tall
Bisects the universe between them wall to
    wall
Made of crystalline dumb despair
And each with a cap of boredom screwed
Each day so tightly round the skull
It hurts, it screeches dull dull dull

Escape is an unlikely thing now
From a going-to-death neither foresaw
Recognition, a slow-sliding worm
And nothing ever was done to turn
Away from that giant sucking leech
The leech is filled, the spirit anaemic now
Too weak
Even to crawl
Or reach
For a better kind of death

Santa Eulària des Riu, Eivissa, February 2018.

This is one of those poems that arise spontaneously, and while imperfect, are best if they stay just as they are. It derives from a messaging conversation on the phone with a good friend ahead of a poetry-music-philosophising gathering[4]...

What Shall I Bring?

I asked Majid what shall I bring

He replied most anything

A silver charm, a golden ring

A plate of cheese, something to read

A quiche, a cake, a salad

A hug to make me glad

A song or poem, a jug of wine

A rhyme, a tune sublime

A moment of your time

Your friendly smile

To share with us a while

A friendship to cherish

A joyful, heartfelt wish

A path to walk together

A thought that lasts forever

A warm sunbeam

A diamond dream

The possibilities go on

So take your pick

But just make sure

You bring Eilene

---

4   So I must give due credit. This poem is the work of Majid Rozei and Robert Hale, 2018. And when I say "philosophising", what I really mean, of course, is talking nonsense.

Eivissa, February 2018.

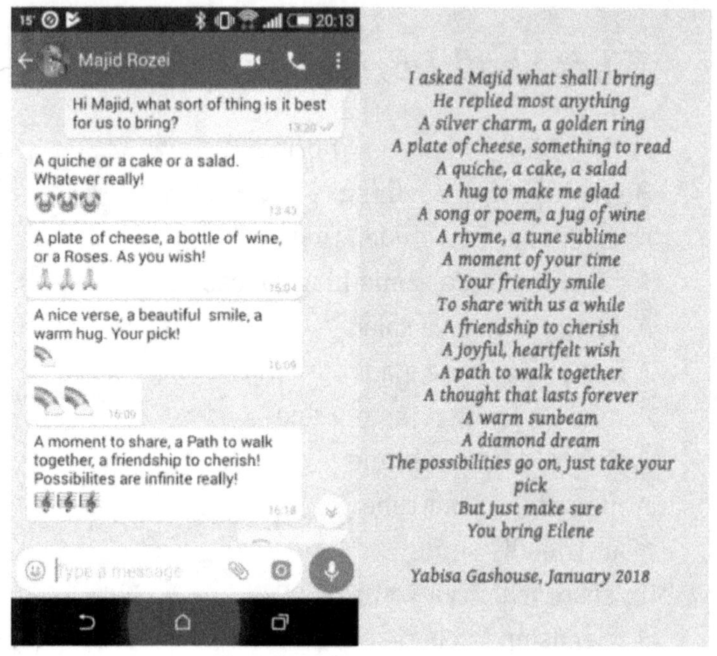

I asked Majid what shall I bring
He replied most anything
A silver charm, a golden ring
A plate of cheese, something to read
A quiche, a cake, a salad
A hug to make me glad
A song or poem, a jug of wine
A rhyme, a tune sublime
A moment of your time
Your friendly smile
To share with us a while
A friendship to cherish
A joyful, heartfelt wish
A path to walk together
A thought that lasts forever
A warm sunbeam
A diamond dream
The possibilities go on, just take your
pick
But just make sure
You bring Eilene

Yabisa Gashouse, January 2018

A spring night among like-minded friends...

Bewitched Night

Bewitched night, star light
A breath of spring charms the air
All good friends around with talk
And laughter; simple food is brought
Good wine put on the table
Friend Majid tells a fable
Makes us laugh; and Pere on guitar
Plucks a string, begins to sing
The world winks through its veil
Then argue nonsense, trade ideas
Read poems wrought of love and tears
Spirits caught, connections sought
And Youri tells the saddest tale
Then smiles so wide
The brightest smile
All too soon the evening's old
Night's magic tale is told
But one more song now for the way
And may we meet another day
When the planets and stars are right
Bewitched night, star light

Santa Eulària des Riu, Eivissa, March 2018.

In the spring of 2018 I was involved in setting up a small scale project to promote home grown poetry in Ibiza[5]. The idea was to stimulate interest in poetry and writing poetry. We adopted the slogan "Poetry Is Cool", and I wrote this little poem to encourage people to write and submit their own poetry...

Poetry Is Cool

Poetry is cool
Anyone can write it
It speaks the language of the soul
You can even sing or shout it

Find the words to carry your thoughts
Write them down with passion
It is so cool, all people ought
Who cares its not the fashion?

You don't need to follow the rule
Ditch logic and your reason
Travel the currents of the soul
And write it down with feeling

To rhyme or not is no big thing
Just give it rhythm and vibration
Make words dance and paint and sing
Be proud of your creation

So come on people join with me

---

5   Our web and social media identity is Yabisa Gashouse (Facebook and Tumblr: yabisagashouse; Instagram: @yabisagashouse). Our first anthology, *A Crack Between the Worlds: Poems from the White Island,* was published in January 2019 by Yabisa Gashouse Books.

Write to be heard, write to be free

Write something for the world to see
Pray tell...
What will your verse be?

Santa Eulària des Riu, Eivissa, March 2018.

The persecution of the Rohingya people in Burma, and the seeming reluctance of Aung San Suu Kyi[6] even to acknowledge the fact, leaves a big black stain on the copybook of humanity...

Rohingya Father, Rohingya Mother

Rohingya father bleeds to earth his life
Blood dispersed through paddy rice
Even now, hearing cries
Rohingya husband tries to rise, in vain
Rohingya wife is raped again, again
She cries for pain, and burning shame

Rohingya mother cries for fear, her tears
Moisten the floor on which she lies, she tries
But cannot reach her youngest child
Rohingya daughter takes
Rohingya son in hand, she makes
Escape and runs
Runs, from Rohingya land
Behind, Rohingya village burns in flames
Rohingya land? There's no land by that name
Rohingya sister walks the smouldered ground
Where fourteen hundred thousand
Other Rohingya feet
Flatten the path in searing heat

Rohingya brother drinks from stinking ditch

---

6   Myanmar's "de facto leader" (at the time of writing) and a Nobel Peace Prize laureate.

Where Rohingya auntie washes skin of filth
Rohingya uncle's bloated body rots
Beside the long Rohingya line of exodus
Snaking miles on end across
The meagre sun-baked land
To the other side and then
Rohingya hundred thousands cram
Into the wretched border camp
Earth bare, rice foul, the damp
Air foretells the coming rains
Shelters of plastic sheet on bamboo beams
In agonising pain Rohingya baby screams
Cholera wrings her guts
As clouds obscure the sun
Rohingya shelters sink in mud
The beating rains are come

Meanwhile...

State Counsellor, flower in hair
Nobel plaudits all stripped bare
Right now, right there
It is a naked lie
"De facto head of government"
Graciously attired
In Burmese dress, but stricken
Suddenly deaf and blind
Strategic cowardice the disease
Acceptance of the vilest crimes
The powerful to appease
It's a necessary evil
Forgiven by the common people

Moral compass gone astray
They say
But they're just Bengalis
Anyway
Many temples must be built
Atone for any guilt
But if they suffer any harm
There's no due call for alarm
It's just Rohingya karma
That's them, but we
Are decent peaceful
Buddhist people

Santa Eulària des Riu, Eivissa, March 2018.

Is there anything higher, greater, or is this as good as it gets? I am agnostic in spiritual matters[7]. But for me, to live life "as if" is the only way to live...

Survivors

Let us go fearless, you and I
We are survivors
Of the steepest odds
Of most perilous paths
We have made it through
Did you know, my friend?
Five hundred million sperm cells ran the tide
For a fragment of chance
For a splinter of light
For an instant unique
Single and unrepeatable
In an endless ocean of dark
When creation: dramatic
Mysterious, dangerous
Sacred event
Hurled us swirling roughly outwards
Through the well-spring of existence
Into this tumbling river of life
Unpredictable and shifting
Where a choice to go
With or against the flow

---

7   Many people, even educated people, have difficulty with this concept. A lot of people assume "agnostic" is the same as "atheist". Not so, they are quite different. Atheism means a positive decision not to believe. Agnosticism means you acknowledge that you do not know. But even knowing that, it seems to be confusing to some people that one can do this!

Rests on the razor edge of fate

Let us go intrepid, you and I
We are veteran campaigners
Of birth and illness
Accidents, injuries
Mistakes, misjudgements
Trials and losses
Fears, falls, hurts, defeats
Yet here we stand, my friend
Yet here we walk

By pure chance, or mysterious design
And fate walking with us
Silently, by our left side
To take our less-than-half a chance
To walk the jagged stone-bound path
Each step exemplary, unimpeachable,
Exceptional
Each step making the ordinary extraordinary
And the extraordinary ordinary
As far as we shall go

Let us go to climb, you and I
High on the mountain side
I would walk with you a stretch
In silence, single file
You before me, no,
I before you!
So that should I fall
You would step in my dust
And thus I may wish you well

Intrepid friend
We have known, have we not
That in the end we are alone?
Look there above to the high saddle
That is where we shall part
You for your peak, I for mine
And if on your path
You feel dust against your skin
Blown on a warm dry wind
Breathe deep
It is only I again
Wishing you Godspeed
As you would wish me
We will know sadness and we will know joy
But we know, do we not?
Your dust will always have power over mine
And mine over yours

Let us flow like the waters, you and I
From the sea we were born
And to the sea we shall return
Even by this path to the peaks
We may never reach
Yet no matter
In consciousness
We will have tried
We will have journeyed
We will have walked the best road
We will have fought the best battle
We will have become worthy again
Before the return
Washed from the path

Filtered through earth
Carried by tumbling torrents
Swept by great rivers
Born out again from estuary mouths
To our parent sea which begot us

But let us journey on in awe, you and I
Let us wonder and marvel at what is
And what might be
Might it be we have another kind of chance?
Another spark of light in an endless sky of
dark?
A mightier mountain to climb than this
Unseen in the mists beyond the smaller peaks
That yet we hope to gain
Unreachable except
By true survivors?
Could you, miraculous friend
Win through again to another side?
Having made your mountain top your own
Then suspending all belief
And reckoning your odds
At less than five hundred million to one
But choosing to journey ever on
Choosing to live life 'as if'
And only because
Living so, failure
Is an unimportant matter
Just because
What other life is there
Worth a name?

Santa Eulària des Riu, Eivissa, March 2018.[8]

---

8   First published in Poetry Quarterly, Summer 2018, Prolific Press, 2018.

On one of my walks, along a steep rocky gulley, I encountered a large boulder, and for no particular reason I wrote this on it...

Touching Me

A thousand hands have touched me
As they passed by
But touching me is no light matter
For we will always be connected
Will you touch?

Sant Mateu, Eivissa, March 2018.

What if the hills were alive? Aware? The rounded hills of Ibiza, in the winter and early spring, if the day is not sunny, can be dark and brooding. One of them spoke to me thus...

The Hill

Feeling.....
           Feeling.....
                      Feeling.....

A feeling.....
           What?
                      A thought.....

Heavy.....
           I know.....
                      I know heavy.....
                      now.

I know such heaviness.....

Crushing heaviness.

But this came slowly.

So, so, so..... slowly.

Now I feel it has always been this way.

Now I feel it was not always so.

The awakening is so gradual I cannot tell.

I remember dreams.....

Dreams of lightness and nothing.

Dreams of lightness and peace.

Dreams of peace and nothing.

Then I remember other dreams.....

Dreams of great upheaval, of pouring forth.

I am forgetting them.....
                    forgetting them.....
                                    forgetting.

I feel my weight.....

More and more and more.

But there is movement now, too, vibrations.

There is warmth now, too, lying on me.

These are new things.

Somehow these new things are apart, not
        within.

By them, I know my stillness, my slowness,
        cold.

Things within.

The things within are still.

The things apart change.

By them I know time.....

So much time.

I am...

The stillness,
                    the slowness,
                              the cold,
                                    the weight.

I feel…..

Time that passes.

So, so, so slowly.

It is almost as if...

I were time itself.

Sant Mateu, Eivissa, March 2018.

The wind has always struck me as being a very mysterious thing...

The Wind

Poet, you would tell about me?
Eeeee... How long is your book?

What to say? I change
Riding high on feeling's wings
Or they on mine, we are the same
I whistle, I scream, I sing
I am the mood, I am the time
I am the note that jars or chimes
I am the breath upon your skin
I am the balm, I am the sting

I am the scent in your nostrils
I am the sound in your ears
I am the four directions
I am your hopes and your fears
I seize the banner you hold so brave
Then spin you round, make you afraid
Make you mad and make you rave
Or push you down into the ground
And cover up with dust your grave

I can shift the desert sands
Dry all life from the land
Then turn the air electric
And bring the blessed rains
I can summon twenty metre waves

Mountains made of sea
Then charge through their valleys
Howling mad with glee

Wind of fortune, wind of chance
Wind of fate and circumstance
I make the difference, I make the fate
Upwind or down
A kill or an escape
I am the difference, I am the change
Ill wind or fair, familiar or strange

So don't you rely on me
I am volatile
Temperamental
Sometimes extreme
I travel light
Unencumbered by your needs
I am not like that stupid hill
That hardly feels a thing
That can tell you even less
I can tell you so many things
Eeeee..., poet, how long is your book?

Who gently swayed the fronds of palm
The night your Christ was born
And when he hung, limp, upon the cross
And cried forsaken to the blackening sky
Who carried the gathering storm
But I?

I flew with Genghis' hordes across the steppes

Carried the flies to feed on corpses left
But see the green grass growing on the plains
Where the nomads' ponies graze?
Its seed I carried in my hair

Scents of spice 'cross the Indian sea
Drew Arab boats on a hot fair wind
That was me!
Sometimes I took them far off course
In fields of fog too thick to see
The wind was ill
That too, was me!

Who brought the snow that fell so thick
On Russian fields where millions fell
In icy mud and frozen drifts
Then brought again the springtime's thaw
Releasing warriors' bodies
Unto their mother earth once more
But me?

From Hiroshima and Nagasaki
I blasted hot and fast
In my hands I took the deadly dust
And cast it wide about
But then in spring I caught
The dragon's wings, which spread
Northwards through the bleeding land
A wave of blossom from the south

I change. I am so many things.
Would you tell of me?

Eeee... poet, has your pen got wings?

You do not recognise me yet?
We can get personal then
Remember me, remember!
Think back, think back to when...

You sat in the sun by the priory pond
Who gently stroked your cheek
Ran silky fingers through your hair
And carried on her back
The other children's laughs and shrieks
Only for your ears to catch
But me?

Remember who stalked you, tracked you
down
Found you in the bright birch wood
The undergrowth bowed in a shivering line
When I ran straight to you where you stood

Remember atop the Atalaia mount
One who scolded cold and loud
Just when the summer solstice sun
Sank, blood-red, behind
A brooding bank of cloud

Who was it that kissed your back
With a breath soft as a lover's lips
One gentle September? Poet -
Do you remember when?
You wrote a poem about me then!

Who rippled the slate-flat sea in summer
When the moon sailed like a blazing ship
Over the Lizard's back, but me?
Who changed the mood from sweet to bitter,
Who changed the night? For whom
Your poem tried, but failed, and died?
For whom, but me?

I change, I never stop
From the world's edge until the end
You will never catch me up
Eeee... poet, do you have ink in your pen?

Poet, do you see?
How would you tell of me?
I am the mood, I am the time
I am a note that jars or chimes
I am the difference, I am the change
Wind ill or fair, familiar or strange
I run from the worlds ancient edge
And rush towards another age
Eeee... Poor poet, would you tell of me?
Have you room on your page?
Try then, try it if you will
What of value will you tell?
You might just as well
Ask that stupid dullard hill

Santa Eulària des Riu, Eivissa, April 2018.

The Sun has been worshipped by humankind since time immemorial. For good reason...

I, Sun King

I burn in thee
But I do not burn for thee
I give to thee but I do not serve thee
I am life, I am master of all I see
I am King!
I burned so long before your beginning
You cannot even think how long!
I will burn countless aeons after your end
It will be for me as though you never were -
Like a spark quenched by forty thousand
oceans past
A scintilla of power ceded again to me, the
King!
For I am the spark, I am the time, I am the fire
in the sky
I am King who burn through every created
thing
Call life and death on every ephemeron
I am the fire which burns your world
But even I am a transient thing
My flare too will die
All things cease to be
Burn up, burn out
What then?
Not even I can know that
For now though
I burn in thee

I am King!
For now

Santa Eulària des Rio, Eivissa, April 2018.

There is beauty all around if one looks...

Ambiguity

In truth, I never liked this drab and petty town
In truth, I find such beauty here
In truth, our absoluteness lets us down

A small town in north-eastern Italy, April 2018.

In my first collection of poetry, *No Better Time Than This*, I present a trilogy of poems called *The Gift, Ordinary,* and *Extraordinary.* The poem below relates to them. Much of life is a matter of perspective. There is unfathomable mystery behind all things...

Curving Round the Universe

Soaring through the universe
I reach and catch a beam of light
Then riding on the purest curve
Go arm in arm with it in flight

All becomes still within
I myself am time
Incorporate again I ride
A mighty beam in line

Curving to immensity
With shafts plunging below
Converging to infinity
In incandescent glow

I cast my gaze wide about
And this is what I see
A trillion fiery cartwheels
Gyrating endlessly

I curve around the universe
At the speed of light
I curve around and back again
And this is what I find

A gift to shift my line of thought
A crystal clear mind
A poem most sublime which turned
November's rain to wine

I cross the universe and find
This to be the play
An extraordinary verse behind
Each ordinary day

Santa Eulària des Riu, Eivissa, April 2018.

The line between wholesome frankness and arrogant presumption can be fine. Perhaps the difference is the size of the speaker's sense of self-importance...?

Please Don't Say You Tell It Like It Is

Please don't say you like
to tell it as it is
because that is what you say
but what you don't say is
you care nothing for their feelings
and what you don't realise
when you say it's not your problem
that they can't take the truth
is how absurd it is to think
with all except the simplest things
(and even here are bits
which sure as hell you missed)
that what you say is as it is
is anything but the angle
of your slanted gaze.
So don't let me hear you say
as if it were a badge of praise
you tell it like it is -
wind in your neck and
don't be so damn pompous,
it makes me so damned pissed.
Off.

Santa Eulària des Riu, Eivissa, April 2018.

Many are the escapees we meet along the way. But sometimes escape means movement on a different plain. Clearly I am clearly still working on it...

The Escapee

Probably in some way
Like you and him
And her and them, I am
A fugitive, a refugee
High flying or low creeping
We are that much the same
And there is no escape that I can see
By any normal means

In the square of a middle-sized market town
The people stare when the shoes on your feet
Are different from those in the windows of the
      shops
Or your face is not from the standard mould
They do not cross the road when the little man
      is red
Even when no traffic is coming
And the cars do not stop at the zebra crossing
Even when people wait to cross
A trip to the shopping mall on Sunday
      morning
Is the project for the week
A town dropped centuries ago from the flat
      grey sky
Onto the flat brown plain
Where the people say

(Never having ventured very far away)
This is the best place in the world

So from this market square
In the best town in the world
I ran far away

Among all pretty hills and valleys
Of flowing waters sparkling in the sun
The light reflected shines so bright it dazzles
Deflecting eyes from many little lies
And eager exiles come in boats
Roam the valleys and the hills
Unwitting bound for other grinding mills
Rose sellers by the village path
Smile bright with seven-coloured eyes
But their smiles are crooked
Seductive air, fluttered whisperings
Essence of thyme dances through the
          glade
But the jade water maiden's troth is lightly
          made
Stained glass splinters tinkle as they fall
Down the church's crumbling walls
While little piles of rocks salute the sacred
          mount
Rising unaware through iridescent mist
And the new preacher blows a kiss
Then runs to land a blow
To the heads of creatures of the unloved kind
While the word book resonates, it's binding
          mesmerising
The kaleidoscope chameleon standing on it

Blinks an eye
Licks up a pretty butterfly
Casts a coin into the well
Pays for a day's illusion
Of the best place in the world

So from those valleys and hills
I ran far
But not away
And am running still

I run to imagined farther corners
I sink to dreamt-of deeper channels
I fly to hoped-for outer reaches
I travel not one inch in space
Yet I am on the run
The companions few but good
Along the way
This is the glorious paradox
There is perhaps escape
But not by any normal path

Santa Eulària des Riu, Eivissa, April 2018.

For a friend of mine...

The Music Man

The music man writes his song
When the light is low and the winds are strong
A song of life and myths retold
In ageless themes from times of old

With an old guitar the tune he strikes
Breathes a note through a thin reed pipe
Both fashioned by the cosmic sum
Where hands and heart and mind are one

He takes his lyre up from the stair
Enchantment gathers in the air
A spell is spun, the rich tones flow
As he weaves them with his magic bow

The music man sings his song
When the moon is full and the evenings long
The people dance as the stars come out
And the music man spreads joy about

Santa Eulària des Riu, Eivissa, April 2018.

"In the beginning was the Word..." (John 1:1). There are two ideas behind this poem. The first is this. Ignore the Christian context of the above quotation. Imagine instead that there were a kind of intelligence at work in the universe, at a higher level than the intelligence of individual beings. "The word", I think, would be a perfect metaphor for such an intelligence. The second idea is that language is under inflationary pressure as never before. Words which once had heart and meaning are diminished to mere containers for empty thoughts...

The Word

In the beginning was the word
It as so very tiny then
A droplet of a droplet of morning dew
Unnoticed
On the cold surface of the world

Droplets met and merged in one
So very fast and then
Pouring ever outwards cast
Great waves far abroad
Shaping forms where once were none

The word flew on a rising wind
Of meaning and intent
Chiselling sense from chaos
A winged worm whose fiery breath
Sprang blooms on barren boughs

The word soared in on the back of a bird
Diving from empty sky
Inspiring awe and action

A marvel for our eyes to behold
Wonder of wonders to unfold

Once the word was great
It had power
It spun magic
It could conjure up the jinn
And mould the fates of men

Ancient tablets, papyri
Great books, sagas told
Inscribed in stone and blood and ink
By hands with a mind to eternity
And the poet bold

Saw the word was precious
Tied his hand to the word
Always searching
Always failing
But always loving the word

Giving it his heart
Giving it his mind
Giving it his hand
The poet tried
The poet always failed

Sometimes the word is a shy mare
Sometimes a running bull
Sometimes touched but never tamed
Waiting, stalking, coaxing, wrestling
Would that it were caught!

Now the world spews out the word
The word it does so little know
The word of much diminished worth
It is but a social tic, a tool
A toy to entertain the fool

The world is careless with the word
It goes by without note
Like a single mark on a rain-stained glass
And few can see as wise Rumi saw
Immensity reflected there[9]

Santa Eulària des Riu, Eivissa, April 2018.

---

9   "You are an ocean in a drop of dew, all the universes in a thin sack of blood. What are these pleasures then, these joys, these worlds that you keep reaching for, hoping they will make you more alive?" (Rumi)

Love, I think, is an acceptance of life that is all encompassing. But that includes pain and death...

The World Is a Tiger

I love the world so much
I lust for her
I long to smell the perfume off her skin
See the sun filtered through her hair
Watch the mist fall around her shoulders in
      luscious curls
When she wakes to the day
I long to feel the prickle of electricity in her
      aura
As her thunderheads roll in
Towering and magnificent
From her unending plains
To ride the great waves breaking on her shores
Tossed naked on her sands
To melt my body in hers
I want to suckle from her for my mortal time
As a child its mother
I want to hold her body for my mortal time
As a man his lover

I love the world so much
In her beauty, her mystery, her awe
Even in her harshness
Because loving her means loving all
The pain just as the pleasure
The bloody wound as the silky caress
The hunter as the hunted

The death as the new life
Because this is the story of our time

I love the world so much
I love her as a Bengal tiger
Such is her beauty, her mystery, her awe
Her wildness, her power, her danger
Life is the killing embrace of her all
Our moment of raging flame
Our moment of vital drive
On time's vast unbroken cycle
To fight for life is love
But if fate ordained the time had come
To lose the fight with honour, and yield
Is truest love
That is the price to pay for love

And yet
As yet
I cannot love the city streets as I love the
        wooded ways
I cannot love the shallow runs as I love the
        deeper pools
I cannot love my love's defilement as I love
        her untamed splendour
I cannot love the chatter of the crowds as I
        love the roar of the wind off the sea
And in truth
I would regard the shark rather differently to
        the tiger

And so
As yet

Though I love the world so much
My love is incomplete

Santa Eulària des Riu, Eivissa, April 2018.

When the words won't come...

Writer's Block

I can't find the words
The words won't come
The words won't flow
I can't find the words
The words won't come
The words won't flow
I can't find the words
I can't find the words
The words won't come
The words won't flow
Bring earth to lay my path
Come wind to carry my mind
Come trees to breathe your life
Come sunlight to warm my mood
Come rolling waves to stir things up
Come flowers to colour my thoughts
Come the night to ask hidden questions
Come the moon to make me a little mad
Come my lover to exult in our mortality
A flask of wine to spice my blood
I will find words

Santa Eulària des Riu, Eivissa, April 2018.

Why follow the crowd..?

Most People

Did they ever say...

That's an odd way to think about it?
That's a strange thing to believe?
It's mad to want to do that?
What a bizarre way to behave?

Did they ever tell you...

Most people wouldn't say that?
Most people would not agree?
Most people wouldn't do that?
Most act normally?

Did you ever tell them...

Most people worthy models?!?
You gotta be kidding and how!?
You never were most people?
And you ain't gonna start now!?

Santa Eulària des Riu, Eivissa, May 2018.

Sometimes I try to see the human race as though I were looking from a distance: as an odd form of life living on a far planet. In that state of mind (or from that point of view), one can abstain from moral and ethical judgements for a while, and the doings of mankind seem to diminish in importance. It's a manoeuvre that one can only healthily maintain intermittently, as one is, of course, a human being. I find the trick is to learn to zoom in and out...

Relativity

If you say the sun
revolves around the Earth
and that the world is clearly flat
they take you for some
religiously perverse
fanatic wacko crack

If you call the act abhorrent
But the actor only human
and wickedness a relative thing
in the longer, broader scheme
they hold you in contempt
as morals are absolute
to the normal being

So why is the wider view
acceptable in space and time
but contemptible in the herd?
And how is a relative stance
in physics all very fine
but otherwise not to be heard?

Looking from within

I walk a flattish ground
The sun comes up goes down
What could be clearer?
Looking from without
I see the earth is round
And its the sun we go around
What could be clearer?
Looking from the borderline
I see a dented sphere
With ups and downs
and flat bits on the rounds
What could be clearer?

Look from a distance.
Look from within.
Stiffness is darkness.
Fluidity is king.

Santa Eulària des Riu, Eivissa, May 2018.

Protect yourself from dogmatists and demagogues at all costs...!

Soap Box Man

He stood on his soap box finger-wagging
All charisma, force and eloquence
Marking each point with a finger-stabbing
Jaw-jutting alpha stance
Indignant, wrathful, thin-air jabbing
Maniacal finger dance

And this is what he said
Soap my friends is black or white
It never should be blue or red
Grey is evil, white is right
And pink we shall not tolerate

The crowd in awe, all heads a-nodding
Goat-eyed wonders, each and all
But then a shout: 'Oy, stop your bragging!
Climb down before you fall
Soap Box Man, your logic's lacking
You're colour blind of course

And this was Soap Box Man's reply
Behold my friends an unbeliever!
By all that's black and white
Throw him into that good river
That'll serve him right!

You righteous soap-box pontificator

Of wretched blacks and whites
With all your "Shall not tolerates”
Why don't you take a hike?
Just because your voice is louder
Doesn't mean your right

And thus came the reply
You lowly unclean abomination
Come my people, give me help!
Give this scum his just correction
And they beat him to a pulp

Because my friends soap's white or black
And orange is perverse
Never ever doubt that fact
Or take your just desserts

Santa Eulària des Riu, Eivissa, May 2018.

Until this year there was a beautiful, very characteristic house, down by the marina, with a white tower with a carved seagull on top. Actually Jack didn't build the house, but he did carve the seagull, and did a lot of work on it for the owners. He was very sad and angry when the local council had the house pulled down...

The House That Jack Built

You know the house that Jack built?
The one down by the port
with the quaint round tower
and a seagull on the top
that Jack carved lovingly from wood?

Jack, who plays the sax so beautifully,
is angry -
says it goes with age.
And French, which doesn't help -
his Gallic liver is full of rage.
Especially now -
a truck knocked him off his bike today.

A big man with a face like a thunder cloud,
a cloud tall as a jinn,
as dark as bile.
But when he smiles, a burning sun
breaks from behind the black.
Briefly.
Sometimes.

And the cloud is always there to take it back.
The cloud is pessimist, disgusted.

Because the world is stupid, corrupted,
says the thunder cloud of Jack.
Angry, disgusted, hepatic, pessimist thunder
    cloud.
Society is decadent, imploding,
and the people just like sheep.
Our politicians do not know beauty
while the people walk asleep.
They despise old things
but they love the smell of lucre.

They knocked it down last week -
the house that Jack built,
down by the marina
with the quaint white tower,
and the seagull on top
that Jack carved from wood.
As if they had knocked him down.
I take it personally he says,
the world is corrupt and stupid.
Where is the seagull? I ask.
I don't know, maybe it died.
Jack is angry
But inside he cries.

Santa Eulària des Riu, Eivissa, May 2018.

May is a beautiful time of the year in Ibiza. The *Puig de Missa* is the picturesque hilltop church above the little town of Santa Eulària des Riu. This poem was written in my mind as I walked up the stone steps from the road, then around the church grounds and finally to look out over the river valley to the south-west...

An Evening in May at the Puig de Missa

Cacti and maquis shout
Riotous as drunks
Up the slope to the Puig

At the church lavender,
Rosemary, hug the walls
By nooks where teenagers kiss

Eastward, Magon's Rock juts its head
Beyond the world's edge
Reaching out

Back of the cemetery
Cypresses pray in sombre file
Reaching up

Bells call Evening mass
Townsfolk in dowdy best loiter
In eucalyptus shade

A white stone cross looks out
Across the river plain
A southern breeze plays

As sun downs on a first summer day

Santa Eulària des Riu, Eivissa, May 2018.

70

As sun downs on a first summer day

Santa Eulària des Riu, Eivissa, May 2018.

When you have grown familiar with a place over many years, especially if you grew up there, it winds itself up with you, exerting a ghostly hold. I find there are two kinds of ghosts...

Ghosts That Stay Behind and Ghosts That Come Along

There are ghosts that stay behind and ghosts
    that come along
The ghosts of the place that owns you stay
    behind
Sometimes they call you in their dreams
And when you go back they run to you
But you have to know where to meet and
    when
They are in the trees and the wind
Among the flowers and in the walls
In the scents of the earth and the shades of the
    light
Their kind is always a delight

The ones that come along are fearsome
    demons
They try to bend and break your truth
Make you speak and act their will
Demean your worth
Scare you half to death while you sleep
With dreams of unseen menace
But like all cowards of their kind
Flee if they meet a ghost that stayed behind

Santa Eulària des Riu, Eivissa, June 2018.

A video appeared on the Internet of an Orang Utan in the Indonesian forest (what is left of it), attempting to defend its tree - the last tree not grounded in a wide area of felled forest - against a large mechanical digger...

Man of the Jungle

Earth shakes, shakes, loud noise
Trees crack, break, fall
Big Red Machine
Eats the trees
I am frightened, frightened
The trees are on the ground
All tangled, ugly
Big red machine
Growls, breaks trees
So they fall
Breaks and eats the trees
And growls

Big Red Machine comes
Comes to my tree
Begins to eat
Shaking, shaking
I am frightened
I must go to Big Red Machine
Make it stop, make it stop
Orang-orang[10] all around
Running, shouting
Running shouting

---

10 *Orang* = person; *orang-orang* = people; *orang utan* = forest man (Indonesian/Malay).

Big Red Machine is close
Growling

I am frightened, frightened

But I must go
Go to Big Red Machine
Try to move Big Red Machine
Try to stop its big hard hand
It is hard, cold
It is strong, too strong
I cannot stop it
I am frightened, frightened
I run away
Orang-orang after me
I run, run away
I run away

Santa Eulària des Riu, Eivissa, June 2018.

Nature is a great redeemer of the spirit...

On the Northern Edge

Away
From the fear, the lies and the spite
From the greed, the filth, and the hate
From the mindless and the meaningless
From the wretched march to emptiness
From the deaf conductor's symphony
From the primacy of the "I", the "me"
From tyrannical mediocrity
There is a happy escape

There's a stairway to heaven on the northern
    edge
Of steps rock-hewn and built in stone
And heaven is on the downward side
By winding trails in murmuring woods
Where shadows play through flowered glades
By sparkling seas of emerald hues
With scents of earth and sea and pine
Acute on morning's sweet of air
And power is alive upon the breeze
And power is rising from the shore
You can feel the breath, you can feel it hiss
You can feel it entering every pore
And power plays on the strings of time
And power plays a tune that's mine
I can hear it sing, I can feel it fly
Transforming all before the day
Transforming all upon the way

Even the world itself will change
To a different tilt and a different spin
And as without, then so within

Cala d'Albarca, Eivissa, June 2018.

Falling in love can be quite unexpected...

Sa Talaia, One Summer Solstice

On a cold and lonely mountain top
We stood fast against the wind
She held my wasted body close
Then took me by the hand

We turned to where the sea meets sky
She walked me to the edge
Then pointed to the setting sun
And there we sealed a pledge

Then at the roadside restaurant
She looked to my eyes to see
The stars reflected, the signs were good
For love was meant to be

Sa Talaia, Sant Josep, Eivissa, 21 June 2018.

The Kogi people live in the mountains of Colombia. They call people of European descent "younger brother". The Kogi, like most peoples who live in close contact with nature, are very environmentally sensitive. This poem is inspired by a BBC documentary featuring the Kogi people. These are their words, paraphrased and adapted for the poem[11]...

When Brother Returned

We came to the mountains
When Brother returned

He brought ill spirits
Which killed our children
Swords and fire sticks
Which killed our men
An unchained beast
Which hurt and defiled our women
A merciless God
To crush all rivals

Younger Brother always was destructive
That is why he was sent away
So long ago
From Gonawinua mountain
Where Earth's precious heart
Beats to the eternal rhythm
Of Aluna
Great Mother

---

11 A few words and phrases are reported verbatim as spoken by individuals of the Kogi people in "Carribean with Simon Reeve", Episode 2, BBC2, Thursday 31 May 2018.

When Younger Brother returned
He came from the dark directions
North and west
He travelled on the right side
The side of those who know less

When younger brother returned
He made disorder from order
Mixing up the seven places
Polluting Earth's lymph
Disrespecting Great Mother
Making her weak
Making her barren

We of the mountain heights
Feel close to the lowland forests
Through which our rivers flow
Feel close to the sea
Into which they empty

See how everything is joined
Cut foot, the whole body suffers
Younger Brother does not know
Younger Brother does not care
Younger Brother is wilful
Younger Brother is careless

Since Younger Brother came
Yuluka[12] is disturbed
The rains do not come

---

12 The Kogi word *Yuluka* means "balance".

The rivers are drying
The insects are changing
The glaciers are melting
The world will not return to normal
Until he stops
Until he listens
He has to listen

But Younger Brother does not even hear

Santa Eulària des Riu, Eivissa, June 2018.

I have mentioned that we have a local poetry group. A few months after its inception - I can be an impatient soul - I was disappointed by the lack of engagement on social media. Ibiza was once a bolt hole for artists and writers, and it seemed to me that that scene had all but disappeared in the wake of the DJs, and the so-called "clubs", the "dance music" and the "party" scene. Or maybe they'd just gone to ground. Anyway, I was just about ready to jack it in. So I wrote this...

The Poets Are Gone

The house is empty
The door is barred
The windows boarded over
The poets are gone
Their words once bravely scrawled
Or painted brighter, bolder
Than the ordinary way
On an ordinary day
Are fading from the flaking walls
The poets have gone to the hills
Their pens are dry
Like the torrent beds
Of a parched July
It is said
Their thoughts have stopped
Like smoke in the air
Hanging over dark hilltops
The poets are gone, the house is bare
The lock is jammed with rust
The writing book is dust
There's nothing there
Any more

The poets have gone

Santa Eulària des Riu, Eivissa, June 2018.

But then somebody said, "Hey, I'm interested". And another person said, "What does it matter? If only one person is interested, that's enough". So I didn't jack it in, and I wrote this...

The Storyteller of Isfahan

On a day, to famous Isfahan
A wizened storyteller came,
Set his stool in Naghsh-e-Jahan,
Told patchwork tales the whole day long.

Strolling townsfolk passed him by,
Some paused there for an instant,
One threw a coin onto the dirt,
Not one stopped and listened.

One morn a small boy came and sat.
He listened hour by hour,
Till the storyteller laid his mat,
In the glow of evening's fire.

Then shyly spoke the boy thus:
Why don't the people listen?
The old man looked to the boy's eyes;
Found there not spark nor glisten.

Because my small, inquisitive friend,
As silk's not spun for me to wear,
My stories never were for them.
Who sees will not much hear.

I like your stories, said the boy.

Because my friend, they are for you.
You made them up just for me?
No! They were woven long ago

In my father's father's father's time,
But verily for you were spun.
How did they know that I would come?
I do not know my little one.

And so in far-famed Isfahan
Sat the wise man all day long
On a stool set in the great meydân
Telling patchwork stories to the throng.

Of one.

Santa Eulària des Riu, Eivissa, June 2018.

Sometimes, when leaving, goodbye is not just a platitude...

another goodbye

robin follows me around the garden
hops a step along the bough
cocks her head
sees me better.
twilight's a twin, we are
familiar
with each other's moods
- tonight's is soft -
and the wood pigeons settling in the trees,
coo agreement.
three oaks salute me down the road
one stunted, old and wise before its time
one stands tall and broad, majestic, a king
of its kind, a third
gathering, enfolding, like a mother
and a whole world moves within.
behind the tracks i press the skin of my palm,
through ivy
to the chestnut's old hard warm hide,
feel its beat, it has seen
more vigorous times, but remembers still.
people stare as i turn,
throw back my head arms raised and spin,
appreciating him from other points of view.
back over the lines
big grey she-cat walks across the road for a
stroke.
in the garden a starless sky

shirt off, lie on cool prickly grass, looking up
traffic noise from the main road but OK
earth moving like a muscle beneath my body
while the air holds me in its cradle.
intoxicated but not now on grape.
another goodbye.
all of this means a very great deal
and nothing.
do you know what i mean?

Four Marks, Hampshire, and Gatwick Airport, July
2018.

On the night of 27th/28th July, people lined the waterfront of my home town to watch this century's longest total eclipse of the moon. As a habitual student of human nature, it seemed to me that among the iPhone army gathered there, a sense of wonder had gone astray somewhere...

Eclipsed

A moon announced
V.I.P. moon
Red-carpet moon
On the telly
News presenters
Astronomers
Excitedly
All much ado

iPhone army
On the sea front
Lotus positions
On the beaches
Great expectations
Significant event
Poor moon
Big responsibility

Moon emerges
Shy, private moon
Reluctant V.I.P.
Rises slowly
Blushes, darkens
Hides her face

Merges with the night
Peeps out once more

iPhone army
Shifts, lotus positions
Get up and go
Move on
Mental boxes ticked
Quickly out of mind

Morning after
Looking skywards
Fluttering spangles
Golden brilliance
Dancing all around
Blinding nucleus
Beams fan down
Filter through green-white
Soulful soft

Holding on
Eel grass anchors
Let the water sway
Me back and forth
Watch transfixed
Lazy light show
No news channel
Announced it
No astronomers
Much ado
No iPhone army
Lotus positioned

Nobody here
At all, in fact

Many the time
Is extraordinary
Eclipsed
By ordinary

Santa Eulària des Riu, July 2018.

Some small things about my home...

Island

Little white house among dark hills
Patchwork squares the farmer tills
Pine trees blanketing slope and fold
Whitewashed church on rocky knoll

Fishing boats rock in the dancing light
Boat houses sit round a tear-drop bight
Cliffs climb high from the rocks and scree
Swifts soar fast high above the sea

Santa Eulària des Riu, Eivissa, July 2018.

Early one August morning I lay on the water and let go for a little
while...

Floating (A Meditation)

Floating
Undulating
Becoming the wave
Drifting
Right and left
North and south
Rising, falling
In all combinations
Of x, y, and z
Thinning out
Evening out
Extending beyond barriers
Dispersing over distances
With watchful abandon
Melding with the medium
Becoming the ocean
Becoming the sea
Warmed by the silver sun
Brushed by the cooling air
Meeting, merging
Becoming one
And one becoming nothing
Not in time nor place
Not deep nor shallow
Not here nor there
Just all and everything
And nothing

Then the click, click, click
From two thousand tiny claws
Of a thousand tiny shrimp[13]
That seems to come from inside
Moves back out
Draws me back in
I feel and so I am
The me again

Santa Eulària des Riu, Eivissa, August 2018.

---

13 Sound carries extremely well in water. That high frequency clicking sound that snorkellers and divers are familiar with is believed to come from the actions of countless crustaceans like crabs and shrimps hidden among the rocks and vegetation on the sea floor.

A summer evening on the beach with Clouds Woman. Most other people have left. I go for a short walk in the woods...

She Waits for Me

The sun is down
As I climb the hill
And the moon is half
And the woods are still
And the pine scent calls
As cicadas shrill
And the waves run gentle on the shore
And the rocks are warm under my feet
And a seagull calls and curves to east
And my love waits quiet upon the beach
And my love awaits, so I make fleet

Cala Nova, Sant Carles, Eivissa, August 2018.

Where I live there is a guru to be found under every stone. Take your pick; their stories, and their teachings, are all much the same...

The Great Guru

He does the things he has to do
Bows down, then upwards he will reach
To the sun in the morning on the beach

I don't know how or when, says He
I became such a Great Guru
It's just my Karma passing through

It was a gift, ordained, but all the same, says
    He,
A burden, I accept with customary grace
Serenity washing like pastel paint across his
    face

But I've read how it came to pass
How a young man's life forever changed
On his professional website's "bio" page

How the spirits spoke
To a child shivering in the dorm
And how he was struck in a lightning storm

It knocked him out, but when he woke
He found his senses splinter sharp
Then wandered raving in the dark

For long he could not understand
And the young man turned his hand
To playing in a reggae band

Drink, and drugs, and on the road
Till after a gig in Athens, Greece
He left and joined a band of freaks

Travelling far, seeking truth
Dharamshala, Bali, then Peru
Met wise man, fakir, sage, guru

Studied with all the greatest masters
Absorbed their wisdom, learned their crafts
Their ancient secrets, hidden arts

Now he knew what was that dread
Voice in his childhood head
Trembling in his lonely bed

They said, they moaned, "Awaken us"
Those strange disembodied voices
So it never was a matter of choices

Great Guru (says I), are there are others just
    like you?
The bio is always about the same
Now I'm hearing it again!

Ah, a cynic I see! Says He
(Here a knowing smile)
Open your heart, my poor lost child

Love is all and everything
So light a candle in your dark
Pay good heed, and hark:

This now is everything and all
Else is mere illusion
A towering babel of confusion

A fantasy of the material world
Behold the universe with awe
For all is one, and one is all

But Great Guru, I've heard these things before
They sound quite commonplace to hear
Of copyright you have no fear?

Remember your mortality! Says He
Behold the moon above
Rising like a flying dove

Verily, it knows no wane
How often will it rise to look again
Through this place, for you, in vain?

Wow, Guru, that's cool and sound! says I
I know just where you read that, man!
It's from the book of old Khayyam

Understand! Says he. Most of you is mystery
Unseen, unknown, unheard, unturned
(And here he's channelling Rhonda Byrne...)

I read that, too! I cried (with pride)
It's in "The Secret", but I'll confide to you
She knows how to make a bob or two

All thoughts are energy! What's sent out, says
    He
Comes back, the universe will provide
And then of a sudden, this he cries:

Look to the stars! Scatter your delusions!
The poor get sick from need, the fool from
    vainglory!
And this was nicked, I think, from Bob
    Marley[14]

You have no time, says He, now take
    responsibility!
Behold your death, just round that left-hand
    bend there!
And this was straight from Carlos Castaneda

You read a bit, says I
And speak it, too
Is that not so, O Great Guru?

Well then let the quiet speak! Says He
As that begins, we shall start out, two silent
    birds
The radiant one in me has never said a word

Ah, you've read friend Rumi too! Says I

---

14 Not quite. This is heavily paraphrased from his song, "Stiff Necked Fools". I
hope and believe this would pass as "fair use".

I find, with some surprise
For thirty years old you are so wise

Such common thoughts so deep
Delivered just in the right disguise
With robes and stones and signs

And the change in your tone of voice
And that upward turn of your eyes
So I only see their creamy whites

And what a splendid sight!
An entertaining show
But here's something you should know:

We believe, we live, we are reborn! Says I
So swim in quantum consciousness!
Walk on in pure righteousness!

Hey man, that's good! Says He
How did you learn that stuff?
Says I: Guru, I made it up

So tell me now what you know
You've paddled a stream or two no doubt
But have you tried the ocean out?

What of your great humility?
Deep down do you enjoy acclaim
Warm at the mention of your name?

The importance and the power

To tell them what to think and do
Control their lives, yeah hey, Guru?

Dictate their days, bask in the haze
Of glowing adulation
And glean a pretty remuneration

But Great Guru's not finished yet
Like the moon above, he'll never wane
And now he raves some more, in vain

Take heed! Shouts he. Let us be free
We are all one, but one is two
And two and two are three
While three and three are just too few
You are the bear, I am the bee
Upon the Holy Flea it's true
That even the deaf can see
Thus spoke I, the Great Guru.

Santa Eulària des Riu, Eivissa, August 2018.

Our sense of identity is a curious thing. It has many layers. How often do we think about the deeper reaches?

Aware Beings of the Universe

What does it mean to be of my race?
To be of my church, to be of my faith?
What does it mean to be of my tribe?
To be on the left or else on the right?
What does it mean to be of my colour?
To be of my own father and mother?
What does it mean to be of my gender?
To be a brother or sisterhood member?
What does it mean to be of my station?
To be of my country, to be of my nation?
Many will wonder on lesser questions
But what of the meaning, the rhyme and the
      verse
To be aware in the universe?
What is this "I" and where are its bounds?
This thing that perceives, where is it found?
Wrapped up all within the skin?
Or reaching far past sight will fling?
What is your meaning, what is your force
Aware being of the universe?

Santa Eulària des Riu, Eivissa, August 2018.

While out walking I came across a deep crevice in a rocky outcrop
at the top of a cliff, which fired my imagination...

Chasm Between Worlds

I remember as it were a dream
This crevice upon the mount
This fissure into savage rock
Of deepness beyond count
This abyss unto the mystery heart
This shaft to the unknown
This passage to Eden's earthly bed
This breach in my here and now
This cut into the wall of sight
This chasm between the worlds
To where the flesh meets heart meets mind
And even chance the soul
Though not immortal, just a spark
For precious seconds before the dark

Santa Eulària des Riu, Eivissa, August 2018.

Ibiza seems to exert an eternal magnetic pull on those who once fall for her. But the people who believe they know her well all have their own versions of her. In fact, ever since I came to live here in 1998, people have been telling me as fact, "Ibiza is this, Ibiza is that, Ibiza is like this, Ibiza is like that". If that happens to you, don't believe them, for Ibiza is in the eye of the beholder...

I Fell in Love with Tanit

I fell in love with Tanit[15]
In her cave high on the mount
She plied me with her Godly wine
The colour of the morning sky
Before a summer rain

By the fullness of the moon we loved
Three days in its silken rays
The shifting images now are vague
Reflections on a gentle wave
The wound as raw as blood

White-faced she stood among the pines
Wild hair blown by the wind
Long she looked out from up high
Above the silver sea
The wine jug broken on the floor
The revels but a dream
Her babe sleeps peaceful, it was born
From Scorpios tail they say

15 Tanit: a Phoenician and Carthaginian goddess worshipped in Ibiza in ancient times. Goddess of war, fertility, and motherly love, her cave-shrine is found high on a hillside overlooking the sea near the village of Sant Vicent in the North East of Eivissa.

One night I bathed with a mermaid
In the singing sea below
Then sitting on the empty sand
At twilight looking south
I gazed too long in the face of Mars
Risen o'er horizon's band
Of an orange so bright I felt the glow
Its heat upon my skin
And later Tanit from her cave
Cast me down in rage

Some say she is a warrior
Both merciless and cruel
To some she is a mother
Both mild and merciful
To others still a lover
Wild and free and full
Some say she is a wanton whore
With forty bastard sons
Some say it's either love or hate
She'll take you as her own
Or chew you up and spit you out
And nothing in between

Well I have been her lover
And tell it from a different side
Her faces are the zodiac
A pantheon of gods
As many indeed as eyes that look
But few there are to see
She reflects from many angles
So she'll be true to thee

I love her still when the moon is full
Though her fury knows no bounds
But she loves me too and looks out for me
As I cross the stormy sea

Santa Eulària des Riu, Eivissa, August 2018.

All religions of the world preach love. What is this love?

In Love

Be in love, said the wise woman.

        With a woman? I asked.

God willing, with a woman, too, she replied.
But not only.
And in that case do not confuse passion with
love.

        What then of passion?

Passion may exult in love
but is not itself the love.

        Is love God? I asked.

Not exactly.
But you might say God were the great source
of love,
as the sun is the great source of our light.

        Then what is this love?

I can only tell in words some of its traits.
Love is pure joy of spirit.
Love is unconditionally generous.
Love is out-flowing.
Love is the creator of beauty.

Love is the medium for perfect acts.
Love is out-reaching for another moment.

Can we be in love all the time?

Inside the Love. Yes, we can.

What if we are broken?
What if the joy in our spirit has
left?

There are times when it seems so.
But Love does not die, it just moves behind
to give support, when times are black.
If you grieve, grieve completely.
Love is there, it will bring you back.

(Silence)

Have you more questions?

Not now.

Do you feel the love in my words?

I do.

Are you, then, in love?

I am.

Santa Eulària des Riu, Eivissa, August 2018.

This is a lovely old tale that has woven its way among various eastern traditions through the ages. I have made it into a poem, and added a few small things...

The Cracked Pot

Each day with water from the well
A bearer walked the winding path
Carried in two earthen pots
Across her shoulders on a staff

One of the pots was new and sound
The other old and cracked
It dripped and dripped along the way
On the left side of the track

When come to the mistress's house
Of its load but a third was left
It bowed its head and hid its face
Ashamed at its uselessness

Day after day it was the same
And sadness its soul did fill
The only thing that brought it cheer
Were the flowers on the window sill

Such pretty flowers as those
To any would bring a smile
The water-bearer, seeing this
Thought for a little while

This kindly but plain speaking soul

Spoke thus to the tearful pot
I see the flowers do cheer you up
Where do you think they were got?

I know not where, replied the pot
A beautiful place for sure
Well listen to me, the bearer said
Pick your heart up off the floor

Come hither to the well with me
Enough self-indulgent woe
Fill thee with water, and when full
Look back along the road

Raise your eyes and look about
Look well, Cracked Pot, and mind
You might just surprise yourself
So pray tell me what you find

So on the road back from the well
Hung from its bearer's staff
It raised its eyes and looked about
And then let out a laugh

Look, look! it cried in great delight
Pretty flowers all in a row
The same ones as back at the house
How strange that here they grow!

That's right, the water bearer said
Those flowers come from here
But look again and tell me this

Which side do flowers you see?

Why, they're only one side, the left!
On t'other there are none!
How can it be? Here so fresh
But there as dry as bone

Now, clay pots are not so sharp
So the bearer had to say
Where do you think the water's from
You cracked pot of clay?

And you (turning to the perfect pot)
Bravo, your work is excellently done
But perhaps now you might well stop
Looking so smug from now on!

And thus the cracked pot came to know
A truth that should be clear
That a trait you see as a defect
May otherwise be dear

It never would sad again
For all its water spent
Along the path down from the well
Spreading beauty as it went

Santa Eulària des Riu, Eivissa, August 2018.

Most of the time we don't realise just where we are...

Wonderland

Stop.
Just stop.
And listen.
Hear the breeze rustle the canes.
See them sway.
Moving light and shade.
Feel it stroke your skin.
Tousle your hair.
Realise what it means.
You are aware.
You are.
Just be for a while.
Yourself.
Alone.
Naked.
Yet sufficient.
In wonderland.

Santa Eulària des Riu, Eivissa, August 2018.

Across the alleyway from our second-floor flat is another flat, with a cat. Its owners were obviously out, and it had been shut out on the balcony. It was mooching about looking bored, and I imagined a whole lot of other cats in a similar situation, all mooching about on balconies getting bored...

Those Cats in Those Flats

Those cats in those flats
Do they ever go out
To meet other cats
From other flats
And prowl round about?
Or do they just stay in
And play with a tin
Or a ball of string
Or something like that
If I were a cat in a flat
I'd try to get out
And prowl round about
And fight with a matey
Or meet a cat lady
Or hunt down a rat
And be a true cat
Not shut up in a flat
To lie on my back
And meow and be cute and get fat
And that's that.

Santa Eulària des Riu, Eivissa, August 2018.

This poem is about the theft of the Black Hills[16] from the Lakota and Dakota Sioux peoples by the US government in 1877. Having previously signed treaties establishing the area as Sioux property, the government reneged, unilaterally annexing the territory. Whether or not this had anything to do with the discovery of gold in the hills is a matter for conjecture. Certainly the ensuing gold rush antagonised the native tribes and led to tension between the two sides....

Real Estate

I have never known why they call them black
You have never seen such colour as in those
       hills in the autumn
Or such glowing splendour as theirs in a
       summer sunset
And midwinter they are clothed in the purest
       coat of white
Maybe it is the darkness of the pines against
       the bleak grey sky
Before the snow, who knows? Not I

I could never understand how you could not
       feel it
To us they were filled with spirit
We knew spirit in all things
But among things, those hills were special
Among them, Tokahe[17] came to the surface of

---

16 The Black Hills are a small mountain range rising from the plains in the western part of South Dakota and eastern Wyoming. They were sacred to the Sioux tribes of the great plains.

17 *Tokahe*: "The First" in the Lakota. Tokahe was the first man to step on the surface of the Earth, having been brought up from the subterranean world by a spirit, through the Wind Cave in the Black Hills.

Earth
Among them, we went to be still
Among them, we felt close to Great Spirit[18]
Among them, we found our medicines
Perhaps in very dark hearts the Spirit's light
Is too weak to glow, who knows? Not I

We did not know how one could trade in
        mother Earth
But you promised us these hills for eternity
Then you came for the gold
And took the hills as your own
Offering dollars in return
Some of us fought but you were too strong
And today
Your chiefs' heads stare from the
        mountainside
As if to make that point
Maybe what we found there is of lesser worth
Than your gold, who knows? Not I

I never knew the difference between myth and
        history
But then history spoke
Teaching me an age-old truth
The stronger encroaches on the weak
They stronger one prevails
New gods replace the old
No doubt we did to those who came before
As others will do to you

---

18 *Wakan Tanka*: "Great Spirit" in Lakota. Defying any description, the Great
    Spirit was also known as the Great Mystery.

The world is changed and yet
The world goes on the same
Perhaps it is the nature of spirits without peace
Perhaps I am confused, or you, or we
What is worth more, the Spirit or the gold?
Which gods more powerful, yours or mine?
Who knows? Not I

Santa Eulària des Riu, Eivissa, September 2018.

My daughter (who is a runner) wrote the words in prose, and together we turned them into this poem...

See Her Run

See her run -
Like the mustang on the plains
Running is the journey and the end
She runs for no other reason
Because that is what mustangs do

See her run -
A fresh wind on her face
A quickening of the pace
A breaking of the gait
She senses a journey begun
She feels the thrill, she runs
Her way and aim unknown

See her run -
The road is a teacher of many lessons
Patience
Not to set off at a mighty gallop
For then the pace will wane and die;
Frugality
For she who manages her energies will go far;
To embrace change
For even staying herself
She changes day by day;
To slow the thoughts
In order to learn
To listen

In order to feel the way

See her run -
Today she chooses paths untravelled
Tomorrow the old familiar route
Today she travels far
Tomorrow just around the block
Everything changes, nothing stays the same
For this she is not less than she was before
But more

See her run -
She gives herself to the rhythm
Impelling her ever on
The sound of footfall on the ground
Arms move in time
Balancing the stride
Carry her like power wings
And beat of heart that joins beat of step
Percussive harmony
And the wave that fills the lungs
Of life and vigour to blood and flesh
The pump of breaths hypnotic
The pulse ancestral
And cradled by it
She in turn
Cradles it within

See her run -
Her gesture of greatness, of power
Always, endlessly onwards
Immersed in rhythms

Witness to the world
To everyday wonders
Trees, birds, insects, flowers
In a different consciousness
Living what surrounds her
Living what arises within
The flows and fragments
Thoughts, images, emotions, sensations
Sometimes fast, sometimes slow
Sometimes painful
As if the running breath would rinse her out
Shake her from within
Her footfall on this earth her truth
And her reflection
Returning home a small rebirth

See her run -
Like the mustang on the plains
Who knows where?
She smiles inside
See her run
See her run

Eivissa, May/September 2018.
Copyright © Soledad Hale and Robert Hale.

A simple event in childhood often forms a significant impression, even though the memory of it may be fragmentary. So significant that it may determine a whole facet of our lives, at least so far as we weave a story from it, a story that melds with our personal body of myth...

Girl with a Yellow Ribbon

A little girl at a ribbon stall
Blue, pink or brown?
Yellow he said, to her surprise
And so she took it down

Ever since, her drawings she filled
With that bright and cheerful colour
And ever since, the clothes she chose
Would carry a touch of yellow

The girl with the yellow ribbon in her hair
A thousand steps in the world has come
But when, in the distance, he looks, she knows
She can make a thousand steps and one

Eivissa, March/September 2018.
Copyright © Soledad Hale and Robert Hale.

This old tale from Mesopotamia has been told and retold in various ages, places, traditions, and forms. This is my adaptation of the version from Islamic literature....

The Old Man and the Angel of Death

An old man came to Suleyman's court
His grievances to air, but there
Found the King with the Death Angel
In talk of state affairs
The angel turned his black eye pits
To the man, who, in them seeing doom
Turned deathly pale, felt faint and sick
And the angel left the room

"Friend, what ails you?", asked the King
"I fear to tell, my Lord
But I beg you, Sire, please summon a jinn
Have it me take me now away in haste
To the farthest lump of mud in Hind"
So then replied the King
"Sir, I know not what your cause
But may your wish be granted thus"
And so a jinn was called

In a second the task was done
The old man whisked away
To a lump of mud in far-flung Hind
And it came to pass next day
That the angel came unto the King

Saying, "That man yesterday,
How strange that I should find him here!
When in the book of fate was writ
He should be in the Hind!

"It was ordained when time began
That at break of day this morn
I must go there to find that man
On a lump of mud in the farthest place
Indeed just so I found him, whence
He dropped down on his knees to pray
And gazing deep into his face
I sucked his soul away"

Santa Eulària des Riu, Eivissa, September 2018.

Who hasn't thought about how they would like to die? There is nothing morbid about this so long as we do not dwell upon it unduly. Because awareness of our mortality enhances our experience of this moment of life. May a life well lived bring the right kind of death...

When I Die

When I die
The sun will be just above the horizon
On a clear golden dawn
A green vale will stretch out before me
Rivers and lakes will glisten in the sunlight
With lines of willow trees standing witness
I will sit high above, among pine-clad slopes
And beyond, on both sides
High and magnificent peaks
Will march into the far distance
Then I will stand up on my high ledge to sing,
And I hope I will sing my song well -
My last statement
And a fitting thank you
To this beautiful world

Santa Eulària des Riu, Eivissa, September 2018.

About the Author

"While still on the road, learner, hunter of icicles, drinker of Khayyam's wine, some kind of healer."

Robert grew up in the south of England before seeking his fortune in foreign lands. His home now is on beautiful Ibiza with his beloved Clouds Woman, who keeps him grounded and disabuses him of any notion that he might be in any way perfect. He makes himself useful and earns a crust by providing health care to the local community. He loves to spend time walking the woods, cliffs and coastlines of his island home, and torturing some apology for music out of his mandolin. He loves solitude, bodies of water, forests, observing the beauty and the harshness of nature, and (quixotically) pondering the imponderable mysteries of life. His poetry is inspired by the beauty and mystery of the world around us, the natural environment, the human condition, and the greatest motivator of them all, love. Robert has been published in several respected poetry magazines. This is his second collection of verse. His first poetry book, *No Better Time Than This*, was published in February 2018. Robert's other works include a guide to managing stress, a technical book on acupuncture, and an online guide to the medicinal herbs of Ibiza (under perpetual development).